# Penguins in Peril

Written by Victoria Travers

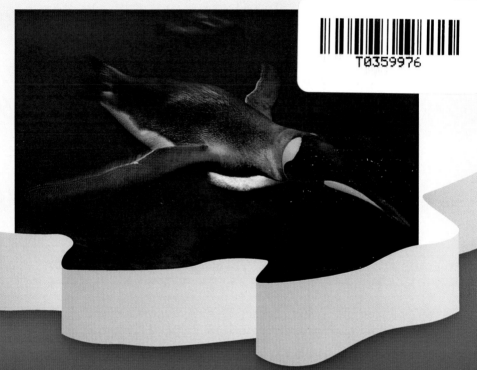

T0359976

## CONTENTS

# Penguins in Peril

Penguins are birds. Unlike most birds, penguins swim through the water instead of flying through air. There are 17 different types of penguins in the world and all of them live in the Southern Hemisphere.

Each of these types is called a species. Some of these species of penguins are in danger of becoming extinct. A species that is in danger of becoming extinct is called a threatened species.

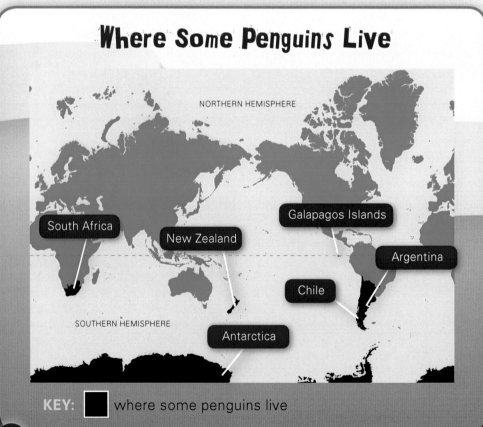

## Where Some Penguins Live

NORTHERN HEMISPHERE

Galapagos Islands

South Africa

New Zealand

Argentina

Chile

SOUTHERN HEMISPHERE

Antarctica

**KEY:** where some penguins live

## Glossary

You will meet these words in this book:

**extinct:** none of this animal are alive any more

**fossil fuel:** a type of fuel that was formed from the fossilised remains of animals that lived long ago

**species:** a group of animals or plants that are the same

**threatened:** any animal or plant which may become extinct and die out in the near future

# Some Threatened Penguins

The most threatened species of penguins are those that live close to where people live.

| Species of Penguin | |
| --- | --- |
| African |  |
| Fiordland | |
| Galapagos | |
| Humboldt | |
| Snares Crested | |
| Yellow-eyed | |

| Where They Live | Are They Threatened? | How Many Are There?* |
|---|---|---|
| Southern Africa | Yes | 140,000 |
| New Zealand | Yes | 6,000 |
| Galapagos Islands | Yes | 2,000 |
| South America | Yes | 24,000 |
| Snares Islands, New Zealand | Yes | 60,000 |
| New Zealand | Yes | 3,200 |

* Penguins can be hard to count so these numbers are estimates

# Threats to Penguins

A long time ago, penguins were hunted by humans for their fat. The fat helps penguins to keep warm when it is cold. People used the fat to light lamps. Now that we use electricity, penguins are no longer hunted for their fat.

While this hunting no longer happens, there are still many threats to penguins. Penguins are threatened because of:

- oil spills by ships
- people fishing for the food that penguins eat
- animals that have been brought by people to the places penguins live
- the earth getting warmer.

oil-burning lamp

inside a fish market

street fish market

# Oil Spills by Ships

Oil is very useful to people. It is used as fuel to drive cars, trains, ships and to run many types of machines. Oil is shipped all over the world in oil tankers. Sometimes these ships have accidents and sink, and the oil spills into the sea. The oil coats the skin of many sea creatures, including penguins.

The oil sticks penguin feathers together. This stops them from being waterproof. If they are not waterproof, penguins get wet and cold, and may die.

A large oil spill covered 20,000 penguins in South Africa with oil. Many helpers from around the world cleaned the penguins day and night with special shampoo. Most of the penguins survived.

helping to clean penguins

penguin covered in oil

oil tanker

cleaning up an oil spill

# Fishing

People like to eat fish, just like penguins. There are many fishing boats around the world catching millions of tonnes of fish for people to eat. The more fish we take from the sea, the less there are for penguins to eat. If penguins don't have enough to eat, their numbers drop because they have fewer chicks.

Some penguins also get caught in fishing nets. Most of these penguins die as they become trapped and cannot get to the surface to breathe.

A fishing vessel hauling in nets.

penguins diving for small fish

# Introduced Animals

Penguins live most of their lives in the sea, but they need to come ashore to build nests, lay eggs and raise their chicks. Some penguins build their nests on the beach, and others make burrows in seashore forests.

Penguins have lived in some places longer than people. When people came to these places, they brought dogs, cats, ferrets and stoats. Many of these animals now live near penguin nesting areas and can eat penguin eggs and chicks. People have also chopped down some of the forests where penguins like to make their nests.

Today, many of these places are protected so that the penguins and their nests are safe from these introduced animals. The safer these nesting places are, the more eggs penguins lay, and the more chicks survive to become adults.

a penguin sanctuary

SLOW DOWN!
PENGUINS CROSSING

KIA TUPATO!
HE KORORĀ E WHITI ANA

yellow-eyed penguin and chicks

nest

# Global Warming

Many scientists believe that the earth is becoming warmer because of the use of fossil fuels. Petrol is a fossil fuel that we use in cars. The use of fossil fuels releases a gas which is thought to make the earth heat up.

Many species of penguins live in and around Antarctica where it is very cold. The colder it is, the more the seawater freezes and creates ice. Inside the ice of Antarctica are tiny plants called phytoplankton. The phytoplankton is eaten by a shrimp-like animal called krill. Krill is one of the main things that penguins in Antarctica eat.

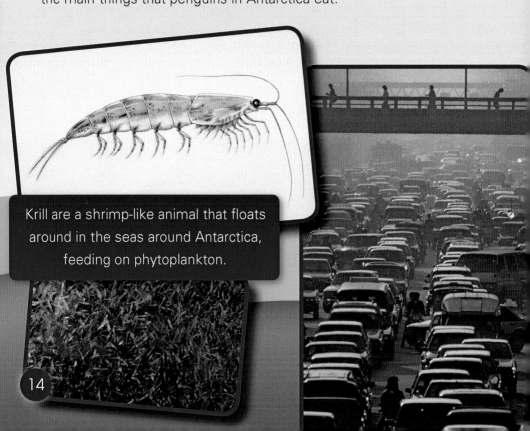

Krill are a shrimp-like animal that floats around in the seas around Antarctica, feeding on phytoplankton.

## What Happens to the Food Chain?

1. When Antarctica warms up, there is less ice and the sea is warmer.
2. When there is less ice, there is less phytoplankton.
3. When there is less phytoplankton, the krill don't have enough to eat.
4. When there are less krill, the penguins don't have enough to eat.

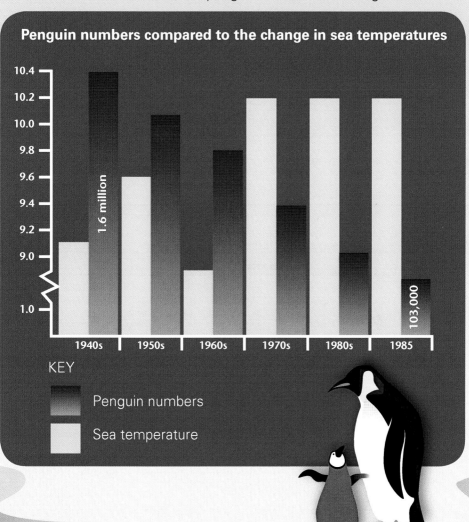

### Penguin numbers compared to the change in sea temperatures

| | 1940s | 1950s | 1960s | 1970s | 1980s | 1985 |

1.6 million

103,000

KEY

Penguin numbers

Sea temperature

# Protecting Penguins

Scientists study penguins in Antarctica very closely to see if their numbers are going up or down. Many countries around the world are trying hard to decrease the amount of fossil fuel that is being used to slow down global warming.

Here are three things that you can do to help protect penguins in peril:

1. Walk or ride a bus to school. The less we drive cars, the less fossil fuel we use and the less the world will warm up.
2. Recycle. The less things we use and throw away, the less we need to make new ones using fossil fuel.
3. Tell other people what you know. They can help to protect penguins too.

# Index

**Penguins in Peril** is a **Report.**

A report has a topic:

> # Penguins in Peril

A report has headings:

**Penguins in Peril**

**Threats to Penguins**

**Oil Spills by Ships**

**Fishing**

Some information is put under headings.

## Fishing

- Fishing boats catch a lot of fish

- Penguins don't have enough to eat

- Penguins are killed by fishing nets.

Information can be shown in other ways.
This report has …

**Labels**   **Captions**   **Photographs**

**Bar Graph**

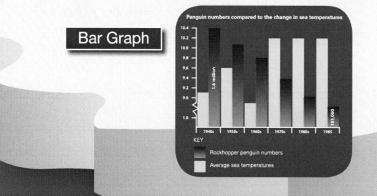

Penguin numbers compared to the change in sea temperatures

KEY
Rockhopper penguin numbers
Average sea temperatures

# ▀▀▀▀ Guide Notes

**Title: Penguins in Peril**

**Stage:** Fluency

**Text Form:** Informational Report

**Approach:** Guided Reading

**Processes:** Thinking Critically, Exploring Language, Processing Information

**Written and Visual Focus:** Contents Page, Bullet Points, Labels, Captions, Illustrations, Map, Comparison Chart, Bar Graph, Index

## THINKING CRITICALLY
(sample questions)

### Before Reading – Establishing Prior Knowledge
- What do you know about penguins?

### Visualising the Text Content
- What might you expect to see in this book?
- What form of writing do you think will be used by the author?

Look at the contents page and index. Encourage the students to think about the information and make predictions about the text content.

### After Reading – Interpreting the Text
- How do you think being able to move quickly through the water could help penguins?
- Why do you think penguins spend most of their lives in water?
- There are many threats to penguins. Which threat do you think is the biggest? Why do you think that?
- Do you think fossil fuels like oil and coal are important for people? Why do you think that?
- What things can people do to save penguins?
- What do you know about penguins in peril that you did not know before?
- What in the book helped you understand the information?
- What questions do you have after reading the text?

## EXPLORING LANGUAGE

## Terminology
Photograph credits, index, contents page, imprint information, ISBN number